There's No Better Friend Than a Sister

Edited by
Angela Joshi

Blue Mountain Press™
Boulder, Colorado

We gratefully acknowledge the permission granted by the following authors, publishers, and authors' representatives to reprint poems or excerpts from their publications: HarperCollins Publishers for "I can remember a time before...," "Every day, when I came home...," and "Fairly often..." from ABOUT MY SISTERS by Debra Ginsberg. Copyright © 2004 by Debra Ginsberg. All rights reserved. Red Wheel/Weiser, LLC, www.redwheelweiser.com, for "Who could say when..." and "We are each other's reference point..." from SISTERS: SHARED HISTORIES, LIFELONG TIES by Elizabeth Fishel. Copyright © 1979, 1994 by Elizabeth Fishel. All rights reserved. Liz Smith for "She's my best friend..." by Nicole Kidman from "Nicole: Standing Tall" (*Good Housekeeping*: November 2001). Copyright © 2001 by Liz Smith. All rights reserved. Kate Coyne for "My sisters are the ones..." by Cindy Crawford and "My sister is the most..." by Sharon Stone from "Sisters" (*Good Housekeeping*: June 2000). Copyright © 2000 by Kate Coyne. All rights reserved. Little, Brown and Company, Inc., and Donadio & Olson, Inc., for "In reality, most sisters..." from THE SECRET BETWEEN US by Laura Tracy. Copyright © 1991 by Laura Tracy. Reprinted by permission of Little, Brown and Company, Inc. All rights reserved. Random House, Inc., for "Visitors to my home always..." and "With sisters you can be ridiculous..." from YOU WERE ALWAYS MOM'S FAVORITE! SISTERS IN CONVERSATION THROUGHOUT THEIR LIVES by Deborah Tannen. Copyright © 2009 by Deborah Tannen. All rights reserved. RLR Associates, Ltd., for "Your sister is your other self" and "Humor lets sisters sail back..." from BETWEEN SISTERS by Barbara Mathias. Copyright © 1992 by Barbara Mathias. All rights reserved. Berkley Publishing Group, a division of Penguin Group (USA), Inc., for "She is your mirror..." from NO FRIEND LIKE A SISTER by Barbara Alpert. Copyright © 1996 by Barbara Alpert. All rights reserved.

Acknowledgments are continued on the last page.

Library of Congress Control Number: 2010904272
ISBN: 978-1-59842-526-0

and Blue Mountain Press are registered in U.S. Patent and Trademark Office.
Certain trademarks are used under license.

Printed in China.
First Printing: 2010

This book is printed on recycled paper.

This book is printed on paper that has been specially produced to be acid free (neutral pH) and contains no groundwood or unbleached pulp. It conforms with the requirements of the American National Standards Institute, Inc., so as to ensure that this book will last and be enjoyed by future generations.

Blue Mountain Arts, Inc.
P.O. Box 4549, Boulder, Colorado 80306

Contents

(Authors listed in order of first appearance)

There's No Better Friend Than a Sister

A sister is friendship, fun, and family
all rolled up into one beautiful person.
She's everything special to your heart –
the one to lift your spirits
and the dearest friend
you'll ever have.

Barbara J. Hall

Sisters make the best friends
because they are family.
Sisters are the treasures of life –
they share their sunlight
and part each other's clouds.
Sisters love us always just as we are.
They bring out life's joys
one star at a time.

Linda E. Knight

There have been at least a thousand times when I have thanked my lucky stars for you.

You are the gold standard that all sisters should be measured by. You are such a wonderful example of how to live a life that brightens the days of everyone around you.

You are a steady stream of support, a reassuring feeling that is always with me, and a gift whose value is immeasurable. You are beautiful in more ways than you know, and you always will be. I am so very blessed to have a sister like you.

K. D. Stevens

When I Look at You, Sister...

I see a remarkable woman
with a kind and caring heart
who is beautiful in every sense
of the word
I see a smile that lights up the room
and laughter that is truly contagious
I see strength and wisdom
beyond anything I have ever known
I see love – pure and true
compassion and thoughtfulness
I see a woman who walks
through this world with gentleness
and grace

I admire you for all that you are
and for all that you do
You are everything wonderful
    in this world
and if I had just one wish it would be
that you could see what I see
    when I look at you

Elle Mastro

The Special Closeness of Sisters

I can remember a time before I was a mother. And, with some difficulty, I can picture a future when I am no longer a daughter. But I can neither remember nor imagine my life without sisters.... My sisters and I have been close our entire lives. The four of us are hardly ever in unanimous agreement and our very different personalities prevent us from ever thinking with one mind. Yet, in our relationships, our work, the face we present to the world, in every day of our lives, each one of us carries some part of her sisters with her. I can't imagine my life without any one of them. Nor do I want to try.

Debra Ginsberg

Who could say when our solidarity began?... Just as it's impossible to point to the very moment one falls in love, so it was with becoming sisters. An accumulation of shocks of recognition, gradual but irrevocable, until we could not imagine how we had survived before.

Elizabeth Fishel

She's my best friend.... Antonia is practically like my twin, even though there's a three-year age difference. We almost have our own language. I mean, we're so close, it's like when you marry one of us – her husband, anyway, said – it's like marrying both of us girls.

Nicole Kidman

My sisters are the ones who knew me when. Everything that's happened since doesn't really matter when it comes to the love we share. That love is unconditional. That's what it means to have a sister.

Cindy Crawford

A Sister Helps Shape Who You Are

Your sister is your other self. She is your alter ego, your reflection, your foil, your shadow. She can represent both sides of you at the same time, thus throwing you into an emotional tailspin. You are different in detail of how you live your lives, but not in substance. Interchangeably, you go in and out of each other's shadows. She is your hero.

Barbara Mathias

Visitors to my home always notice the framed black-and-white photograph of my family. Pointing to the two seated little girls identically dressed, they ask, "Which one is you?" I always respond, "Guess!" They guess right about half the time: I'm on the right, my sister Mimi on the left....

The question, "Which one is you?" is telling. Many sisters ask it of themselves. They can hardly think about who they are without thinking about how they are like or unlike their sisters. A sister is the person you might have been but aren't, by choice or by chance.

Deborah Tannen

In reality, most sisters share only a small portion of each other's lives. But since that portion, during childhood, was so powerful emotionally, often it seems that who we are depends on who our sisters are not. Often, sisters carry each other around inside themselves for the rest of their lives. No matter how geographically distant, a sister can remain the touchstone we use for our own identity.

Laura Tracy

We are each other's reference point at our turning points. And the dance between us is also a delicate balance of influence, between leader and led, teacher and taught, soother and soothed. We alternately give a shoulder and need one.

Elizabeth Fishel

A Sister Is a Gift for Life

She is your mirror, shining back at you with a world of possibilities. She is your witness, who sees you at your worst and best, and loves you anyway. She is your partner in crime, your midnight companion, someone who knows when you're smiling, even in the dark. She is your teacher, your defense attorney, your personal press agent, even your shrink. Some days, she's the reason you wish you were an only child. But most of the time her very existence creates a sense of acceptance, of community, of tenderness.

Barbara Alpert

A sister is a listening heart when yours is broken, a caring word when you need to hear it most. She accepts you no matter how you're handling life; she encourages you just by being on your side. A sister appreciates the little things and notices when you go out of your way; she always reaches out and reaches back.

A sister is someone who is tuned in to what's going on with you; she can sense when you need support and when you need space. She is the friend who's been there from the beginning and who loves you no matter what.

Donna Fargo

We don't get to choose our family;
I just got lucky to have you as my sister...

We spent the first half of our lives together.
For a while, our whole world seemed
to contain only us.
We were like seeds planted in each other's lives,
and we grew up together in sunshine
and in storm.
We shared a special closeness,
maintained a fierce loyalty,
and developed an unshakable trust
in each other.
You are an irreplaceable piece of my history,
an insight into my past,
and a million memories I cherish in my heart.

We were friends then;
we are even better friends now.
We're still learning from, leaning on,
  and loving each other.
We still share a special closeness,
a unique bond, and an unalterable connection.
You know me as only a sister can:
heart and soul, inside and out.
When there's no one else to turn to,
you're always there.
When no one understands,
you always do.
I love you, my sweet sister...
and the heart never forgets its first friend.

Vickie M. Worsham

A Big Sister Remembers...

Every day, when I came home from the school, the first thing I did was bundle [my little sister] Déja up and take her into the unused family room where we kept the stereo and rock her to sleep under the speakers. Because she squirmed if I sat down, I always stood with her in my arms, watching her eyelashes flutter as we moved back and forth. I recorded songs off the radio for this express purpose. We'd start with James Taylor and Stevie Wonder, and move into Billy Joel and through Boz Scaggs. She was almost always asleep by the time we got to "New York State of Mind," but she was so warm and sweet, I didn't want to put her down. I'd hold her like that for hours sometimes, afraid to disturb her peace, afraid to disturb mine.

Debra Ginsberg

What It Means to Have a Little Sister

I'll never forget the day Mom brought Ashley home. I thought she was a gift for me. I absolutely adored her!

Wynonna Judd

In watching my little sister grow, I have learned so much about myself – about living life and loving each and every day. She has taught me that we only live once, so I cry less and laugh more. She has taught me that life doesn't give us more than we can handle and that I can count on her in the times when it seems that way. She has an amazing way of living her life, and I am a better person because she is my sister.

V. Arcoleo

A Little Sister Remembers...

All five girls shared a bedroom, with four beds. Do the math: it meant one of us was the odd girl out, and since I was the youngest that was me.... Every night, I'd have to bunk with a different sister – and here, too, there was a lesson for a lifetime. A situation like that might have messed with my sense of belonging or identity, but that's not how I looked at it. How I looked at it was it brought me closer to each of my sisters. How I looked at it was I had this great gift that none of the other girls had. It might have been a negative, but I took it as a positive. Each night, I'd crawl into bed with a different sister, and as a result we each had a special bond. Instead of feeling like I didn't quite belong anywhere, I felt like I belonged everywhere. It was empowering, really. It made for a series of real, close, substantive relationships, and I had it going on four times over.

Serena Williams

What It Means to Have a Big Sister

The thing I learned from my family and my sister is that you have to look to them for support. At the end of the day, they're the ones that will have your back. People don't realize that having an older sister is so much fun.

Ashlee Simpson

When we were younger, I thought my big sister was the absolute coolest thing on two legs! I wanted to dress like her, walk like her, talk like her, and have as many friends as she did.

I realize now that she wasn't just a wonderful sister – she was a wonderful friend, too. She listened to what I had to say, no matter how silly, and she helped me learn so many things only a sister knows.

We're hardly kids anymore, but I still think she is one amazing sister and one amazing woman. I can't even imagine not having her as my sister.

Rachel Snyder

Sibling Rivalry

In the beginning was your mother. And She spoke the words. And the words were these: "Sisters who love each other do not fight."

And the mother's words were, well, wrong. (Sorry, Mom!)

The truth is this: Sisters who love each other fight all the time.

If you don't understand how a woman could both love her sister dearly and want to wring her neck at the same time, then you were probably an only child.

Linda Sunshine

I have four sisters, and you can fight and get mad, but fighting never breaks the bond of what a true sister is.... I trust that they'll still be there for me even when they are so mad they can't stand me!

America Ferrera

Growing up, my sister was often my rival: fighting over Mom and Dad's attention, over who was smarter and who was cuter, over toys, clothes, and friends. We often took each other's presence for granted, sometimes even wishing we didn't have a sister. Still, there were many important lessons we learned from each other. We learned how to share, how to fight and make up, and how to love each other even when we didn't like each other. I guess you could say we learned what real love is all about.

Isabella Maedl

The Story of Two Very Different Sisters

One is here; one lives there. One is a little taller than the other. Two different colors of hair, two different outlooks on life, two very different views from their windows. Both have different tomorrows ahead. Each is unique in so many ways. Each has her own story, with all the busy things going on in the present. Each has different work to do and different demands on the day. Each has a separate destination and a distinctly different path to get there.

But... for all the things that might be different and unique about them... these two sisters will always share so much. They will always be the best of family *and* friends, entwined together, through all the days of their lives. Their love will always be very special: gentle and joyful when it can be, strong and giving when it needs to be, reminding them that no matter how different their stories turn out, they share the incredibly precious gift of being sisters.

Laurel Atherton

My sister is not like me; she is *another* who started me on the journey to myself. I see some traits in her that I want to claim as my own and some that I accept as different and distinctly hers. We are both flawed and cannot answer all of one another's needs. Yet the comfort of knowing that our relationship will survive despite the differences and imperfections – that our connection as sisters provides a more accurate picture of ourselves... guides us in all our close connections.

Jane Mersky Leder

Karen and I are different all right, but we know each other through and through. I swear I can always tell what she's thinking....

Karen has always been my closest buddy and my best supporter. She's been a big part of my success.... Without Karen around all the time, it would have taken me a lot longer to know who "myself" really was.

We knew we could always count on each other, and together we were an unbeatable team.

Michelle Kwan

The Language of Sisters

Fairly often, Maya will start a sentence and I will finish it for her before she gets to the main point.

"I was going to say that," she tells me. "Why don't you get out of my head and get your own thoughts?"

"I was born first," I answer her. "I had those thoughts before you."

When Maya gets stuck in conversation and can't remember the word or phrase she's looking for (and, as we all get older, this kind of thing tends to happen more frequently), her standard response is, "I'm sorry, I can't get the words right now. Debra's using them all."

Debra Ginsberg

Sisters speak a language that is based on love, not on words. A thousand things can be said through a hug, a smile, or simply a look in each other's eyes. Sisters share the language of two hearts that are closely and intimately bound by friendship, understanding, and caring that never ends.

Natalie Evans

Even when I was suffering through sixth grade, I'd come home and... spend hours on the trampoline with Brandi. Out on the trampoline, we'd talk and laugh about... who knows? Nothing that made sense. That's the best part about hanging with a sister. You're not having conversations with beginnings, middles, and ends. You're just letting unformed thoughts bounce up and down and around and around.

Miley Cyrus

I've watched my daughters weave their lives together until they can read each other's thoughts, make each other laugh or cry, finish each other's sentences. Each knows the other thoroughly, historically, wordlessly, back to infancy and up to yesterday....

Writing this, I realize how sweet and slippery is this word "sister" – big enough to stretch beyond biology and across time; flexible enough to define soulmates and virtual strangers; precise enough to embrace me... my two daughters, and all the sisterhoods in between.

Letty Cottin Pogrebin

Sisters Can Talk and Laugh About Anything

My sister speaks my language.
She knows my whole story,
and I know hers.
Arm in arm,
we've embraced each milestone.
Hand in hand,
we've conquered every challenge.
She is my beautiful soul-sister.
Between us, we've shared
ten thousand laughs
and ten thousand truths.

Maureen Dietz

My sister and I call each other frequently; we're keenly aware of the process of each other's lives, the ups and downs of marriage and work, family and health, the yearly decisions about vacations and Christmas. "What's happening?" my sister says when I pick up the phone. On my desk, I have papers to grade, the first page of a story I'm trying to write. I hear her children arguing in the background, then doors slamming, the intimate noises of family life. Yet for the moment I know she's shut them out, focused totally on me. I feel her waiting, her breath drawing me closer.

I sit back in my chair, prop my feet up on the stool. "You just won't believe this," I begin. And I feel the tug of our secret life.

Patricia Foster

With sisters you can be ridiculous, just like you were when you were kids – even more, because you're acting like kids when you're adults. Picture three women in their fifties and sixties standing before their gathered families and singing – replete with the usual arm gestures – the children's song "I'm a Little Teapot." This is one of the things my sisters and I have been known to do when our extended families get together. We don't often get through the whole thing because we're guaranteed to collapse in laughter before reaching the end.

Deborah Tannen

Humor lets sisters sail back to childhood, when the adults didn't have a clue what was so funny at the dinner table or behind the closed bedroom door. The private jokes put us on equal ground with our sisters; it is also a tremendous release.

Barbara Mathias

It's so easy to be jovial around my sister because she knows how to make me laugh – and laugh at myself. She offers me laughter and forgetting. Takes me out of my head. That gives me the extra boost of energy to do the next mile and the next.

Gail Henion

A Sister's Love

A sister's love is like no other. It is history and hope, poetry and reality, challenge and support, laughter and tears. Other loves may come and go, but ours is guaranteed for a lifetime.

Pamela Koehlinger

You know full as well as
I do the value of sisters'
affection to each other;
there is nothing like it on
this earth.

Charlotte Brontë

No words will ever do a sister's love justice. I know you understand what I'm saying. There's no one like you.

Alicia Keys

No one on the planet will ever know you better than your sibling. They know the good parts, the bad parts, and the secrets. It is a very powerful and valuable relationship. Don't let it slip through your fingers. It is like going home in your heart.

Goldie Hawn

The Ties That Bind Us Together

- We have a shared history. You and I can talk about things that no one else would ever understand. We were part of each other's childhood, are a vital part of each other's present, and will be an important part of each other's future.

- We're inseparable. No matter the physical distance between us, we're never far apart. There is a bond of love and trust that no distance could ever break.

- We're social. You are more than my sister... you are the person I can't wait to tell when something good happens and the one who understands me during the most difficult times as well. You are my friend.

- We're truthful. We can share anything with each other – good, bad, and ridiculous. We are always honest and ready to help each other if needed.
- We're expressive. Whether through card, letter, e-mail, or simple conversation, we share every emotion and feeling. And those emotions we share are part of the strength of our bond.
- We have a great relationship. Strong, durable, and enriching, our relationship means more to me than you'll ever know. You have always been there for me, and deep inside, I know you always will be... just as I will always be there for you. I know we will be friends forever.

Donna Gephart

A Sister Is the Friend Who Is Always There

Some so-called friends will leave you lonely when you need them. Some won't return your call when you're down. Some will gladly be there when you're on top of the world, but a sister is the friend who's always there.

A sister is always on your side. If you need someone to understand you, you don't have to look past her. She will call you back, and she'll keep you in her prayers.

A sister will love you when you may not be so lovable. She'll help you any time you need her to. A friend may forget you or have a "selective" memory when you've asked a favor, but a sister is the friend who's always there.

Donna Fargo

My sister is the most loving, generous, compassionate person I know. If she weren't my sister, she'd still be my best friend.

Sharon Stone

Sisters at one and the same time can be girlfriends, listening ears, best friends, shopping collaborators, just plain buddies, confidantes, rivals, and much, much more....

Sisters, whatever you may say or think, function as one of the best support-systems/ safety-nets in a world churned by the chaos of change all around us. Just the fact that a sister will be there is a great comfort.

Robert Strand

Through all the years
and all of life's twists and turns,
I've always known I could
count on my sister to listen and care,
lend a shoulder when I needed support,
celebrate the good times,
understand what was in my heart,
and be a true friend...
but most of all to love me.

Jason Blume

A sister protects you from harm
and is always near when you need her.
A sister brings sunshine where
there are clouds;
she is like a breath of spring
through the storms of winter,
a guiding star in the darkness of night.

Geri Danks

To this day, I depend on my sisters for love and guidance.... If we don't help each other, who will?

Barbara Mandrell

I'll do anything for her. Anything. It makes me cry I love her so much. You know, I think when you have that kind of love in your family, it keeps you very available and trusting of others.

Nicole Kidman

A Sister Accepts You Exactly as You Are

We can be ourselves with each other.
We share family and memories
and know each other completely.
We share secrets and dreams
and accept each other just as we are.
We often know what is needed
without being asked.
We listen and care.
We accept, even when we don't agree.
We're a special combination of
friends and family,
and the bond of love we share is forever.

Barbara Cage

One thing about us, we may not agree with or support what the other one is doing, but we accept who we are.

Wynonna Judd

No one else could begin to understand me the way my sister can, for she is such a part of my history. She knows my faults and insecurities, yet she respects the person I have become. We can talk about anything and never feel the other will judge or condemn. That, to me, is a priceless treasure.

Cheryl E. Smith

I learned I couldn't fool [my sister Patti]. I couldn't be who I was not. I couldn't fake it. She knew me better than anyone. It didn't matter what I looked like with Patti. I could go without makeup, or even tie my hair back off my face, and it didn't matter. A lot of people arm themselves with who they think they should be so that they can become individuals and break away from what they have been in the past. But until you can be completely raw with someone – as happy as you want to be, as loving as you want to be, as mean, as helpless, as bereaved, as scared, as lost – then you can never really feel comfortable in your own skin. I can be that honest with Patti.

Goldie Hawn

15 Great Things About Sisters

- Sisters are a source of joy and happiness
- They're the only people on the planet who really understand what it was like to grow up in your family
- They want nothing but the best for you
- They're as dependable as the sun rising, the grass growing, and the seasons changing
- You can always be yourself around your sister
- Sisters show you who you used to be
- They show you how far you've come
- They help you realize where you have yet to travel

- A sister can laugh with you just as easily as she can laugh at you
- Only a sister is able to finish your sentences after you've only uttered the first few words
- She probably knows more about you than you do
- Anytime, anyplace, she is always up for a game of rock-paper-scissors
- She still loves you even when she's mad at you
- She has been part of the most important moments in your life
- When you've got a sister, there's a piece of you that never grows up

We've Shared So Many Wonderful Moments

The years of love and friendship
 my sister and I have shared
have held so many moments
full of the most fun
I've ever experienced.
It's always wonderful
to walk back into our childhood
and remember all the times
when we were more starry-eyed
 with wonder
than the heavens above us —
when life was full of innocence
 and the best was yet to be.

As I remember all those exciting times,
I think none of them can compare
to our just being together.
If I could go back just once more,
I would throw my arms around
  my sister and say, "I love you.
Thanks for spending so many
wonderful moments with me."

Barbara J. Hall

Sister Memories

We share so many memories – both happy and sad – that we don't have to talk a lot to know what the other is thinking. A look, a sigh, a hint of a smile... that's all it usually takes to get across a message that says "I'm glad today," or "I'm sad today... bear with me." It's comfortable and it's comforting not to have to say a lot.

Patricia Ziemba

In the middle of the traffic
and the scurry,
the carpools and appointments,
I glance in my rearview mirror
and remember us,
coloring in the backseat...
Sister memories make me smile.

Beth Anthony

I find it comforting to have a sister who can remember all the mundane and dramatic things that happened around us as children. I always find it uniquely reassuring to discuss childhood memories with my sister. She's my connection to my past, the only person who can help me remember what happened.

Marcia Millman

A sister is a little bit of childhood that can never be lost.

Marion Garretty

What a Remarkable Sister You Are

There are so many times
when I am in awe of you.

And I want you to know
that I admire you so much!

I admire
the life that you lead and
the kindness that is such a
sweet and natural part of you.

I admire
the way you treat other people.

I admire
how easily a smile finds its way
to your face.

I admire
the work that you do and the
places your journeys take you.

I admire
your dedication to all the right
things and your devotion to your
friends and your family.

I admire
how completely you care and how
willingly you are always there
for the people who need you.

I admire
so many things about you,
and I thank you with all my heart
for being the light that you are...
to my life.

— L. N. Mallory

Thank You, Sister...

For all those times when I never could have managed without a sister like you.

For being such a constant in my life – amidst all the changes the rest of my world goes through.

For being remarkable in your qualities, inspiring in your thoughts, and caring in your heart.

For being the one I will always feel close to, whether we're together or miles apart.

For being my definition of "special," and for proving it over and over again.

Douglas Pagels

Sister, your heart has been the one I've trusted with my deepest truths – knowing they'd remain both guarded and understood. Your heart has been attentive to all that matters most to me – listening to me in comfort and support. Your heart has kept me smiling through all the ages and stages we've passed through – and it has loved me without question or fail all the blessed days of my life.

I thank you with love and gratitude for the countless gifts of your heart – trusting in return that you will always find a home in my heart, too.

Lynn Keachie

We have grown through much together and this I know without a doubt: I love you. No one can make me laugh like you do. No one can remind me of what matters most like you do. No one else can relax me with a phone call like you do. You are my anchor in my ever-expanding life. There is no way to thank you for all the gifts you have given me in this lifetime. So I simply say thank you!

Rhonda Britten

Sister Wishes

I would give anything for these wishes
to keep coming true for us
all our lives...

That we may always be more than close.
That nothing will ever come between
the bond of love we're blessed with.
That we will celebrate our similarities,
honor the things that make each of
us unique, and quietly realize that
every part of the circle of our lives
is a special, precious gift.

That I will always be here for you,
as you will be for me.
That we will listen with love...

That we will share everything that
wants to – and needs to –
be shared.
That we will care unconditionally.

That we will trust so much, and
we will talk things out.
That we will nurture each other's
spirit and warm each other's soul.
That even when no one else knows
what's going on inside...
you and I will gently understand.

And that wherever you go,
you will be in my heart,
and my hand will be
in your hand.

Katie Russell

Sisters Are Forever

Husbands come and go; children come and eventually they go. Friends grow up and move away. But the one thing that's never lost is your sister.

Gail Henion

It occurs to me that one can never grow up with one's sister. In some secret place we remain seven and eight. And yet we are always family, tied by bonds so deep, so invisible.

Patricia Foster

Each morning
when the day begins,
when other friendships
fade or end,
sisters are forever.
Seasons come and seasons go.
Summer rains turn into snow.
But no matter where you live...
or how far you go...
Sisters are forever.

Ashley Rice

I Will Always Be Grateful for You, Sister

The weather changes. The world changes. People and times change, as well. But the one thing that remains forever constant in my life is you, my sister...

How can I ever thank you for being all that you are to me? All my life I have always had you to count on... and even now, with our lives constantly moving in different directions, I still feel the same comfort I've always had just knowing that you are in the world.

We may not be able to spend every day together the way we used to, but you are still the person I love to laugh with and the person I turn to when life's got me down. I want you to know that our lives may change and we may find ourselves changing, too, but we will always be family, and I will always be grateful that I have you in my life.

Elle Mastro

Acknowledgments continued...

We gratefully acknowledge the permission granted by the following authors, publishers, and authors' representatives to reprint poems or excerpts from their publications: PrimaDonna Entertainment Corp. for "A sister is a listening heart..." and "Some so-called friends..." by Donna Fargo. Copyright © 2010 by PrimaDonna Entertainment Corp. All rights reserved. Vickie M. Worsham for "We don't get to choose our family...." Copyright © 2010 by Vickie M. Worsham. All rights reserved. Dutton Signet, a division of Penguin Group (USA), Inc., for "I'll never forget the day..." and "One thing about us..." from COMING HOME TO MYSELF by Wynnona Judd and Patsi Bale Cox. Copyright © 2005 by Wynnona Judd. All rights reserved. Grand Central Publishing for "All five girls shared a bedroom..." from ON THE LINE by Serena Williams wit Daniel Paisner. Copyright © 2009 by Serena Williams. Reprinted by permission of Grand Central Publishing. All rights reserved. Greg Adkins and Marissa Wong for "The thing I learned from..." by Ashlee Simpson from "Ashlee Simpson" (*People Weekly*: January 10, 2005). Copyright © 2005 by Time, Inc. All rights reserved. Rachel Snyder for "When we were younger...." Copyright © 2010 by Rachel Snyder. All rights reserved. Andrews McMeel Publishing, a division of Andrews McMeel Universal/Universal Press Syndicate, for "In the beginning was your mother..." from MOM LOVES ME BEST (AND OTHER LIES YOU TOLD YOUR SISTER) by Linda Sunshine. Copyright © 2006 by Linda Sunshine. All rights reserved. *Girls' Life* for "I have four sisters..." by America Ferrera from "Friends, Sisters & Magic Pants" by Jodi Bryson (*Girls' Life*: June-Jul 2005). Copyright © 2005 by Monarch Avalon, Inc. All rights reserved. Jane Mersky Leder for "My sister is not just like me..." from BROTHERS & SISTERS: HOW THEY SHAPE OUR LIVES. Copyright © 1991 by Jane Mersky Leder. All rights reserved. Scholastic, Inc., for "Karen and I are different all right..." from HEART OF A CHAMPION: MY STORY as told to Laura James. Copyright © 1997 by Michelle Kwan Corp. All rights reserved. Disney•Hyperion, an imprint of Disney Book Group LLC, for "Even when I was suffering..." from MILES TO GO by Miley Cyrus. Copyright © 2009 by Miley Cyrus. Reprinted by permission. All rights reserved. Letty Cottin Pogrebin for "I've watched my daughters weave..." from "Sisters and Secrets" from SISTER TO SISTER, edited by Patricia Foster. Copyright © 1995 by Letty Cottin Pogrebin. All rights reserve Patricia Foster for "My sister and I call each..." and "It occurs to me that one..." from SISTER TO SISTER. Copyright © 1995 by Patricia Foster. All rights reserved. Maureen Dietz for "My sister speaks my language.... Copyright © 2010 by Maureen Dietz. All rights reserved. Running Press, a division of Perseus Books, Inc., for "It's so easy to be jovial around..." and "Husbands come and go..." by Gail Henion from SISTERS by Carol Saline. Copyright © 1994 by Carol Saline. All rights reserved. G.P. Putnam's Sons, a division of Penguin Grou (USA), Inc., for "No words will ever..." from TEARS FOR WATER: SONGBOOK OF POEMS AND LYRIC by Alicia Keys. Copyright © 2004 by Lellow Brands, Inc. All rights reserved. And for "No one on the planet... and "I learned I couldn't fool..." from A LOTUS GROWS IN THE MUD by Goldie Hawn. Copyright © 2005 by Illume, LLC. All rights reserved. New Leaf Press, www.nlpg.com, for "Sisters at one and the same time..." from MOMENTS FOR SISTERS by Robert Strand. Copyright © 1995 by New Leaf Press. All rights reserved. Jason Blume for "Through all the years...." Copyright © 2010 by Jason Blume. All rights reserved. Bantam Books, a division of Random House, Inc., for "To this day, I depend on my sisters..." from GET TO THE HEART by Barbara Mandrell with George Vescey. Copyright © 1990 by Barbara Mandrell. All rights reserved Jeanne Marie Laskas for "I'll do anything for her..." by Nicole Kidman from "A Mission of Love" (*Ladies' Home Journal*: June 2006). Copyright © 2006 by Jeanne Marie Laskas. All rights reserved. Barbara J. Hall for "The years of love and friendship...." Copyright © 2010 by Barbara J. Hall. All rights reserved. Beth Anthony for "In the middle of the traffic...." Copyright © 2006 by Beth Anthony. All rights reserved. Houghton Mifflin Harcourt Publishing Company for "I find it comforting to..." from THE PERFECT SISTER by Marcia Millma Copyright © 2004 by Marcia Milliman. Reprinted by permission. All rights reserved. Dutton, a division of Penguin Group (USA), Inc., for "We have grown through much together..." from FEARLESS LOVING by Rhonda Britten. Copyright © 2003 by Rhonda Britten. All rights reserved.

A careful effort has been made to trace the ownership of selections used in this anthology in order to obtai permission to reprint copyrighted material and give proper credit to the copyright owners. If any error or omission has occurred, it is completely inadvertent, and we would like to make corrections in future editions provided that written notification is made to the publisher:

BLUE MOUNTAIN ARTS, INC., P.O. Box 4549, Boulder, Colorado 80306.